First World War
and Army of Occupation
War Diary
France, Belgium and Germany

49 DIVISION
Divisional Troops
254 Machine Gun Company
15 November 1917 - 23 February 1918

WO95/2787/3

The Naval & Military Press Ltd
www.nmarchive.com
Published in association with The National Archives

Published by

The Naval & Military Press Ltd

Unit 10 Ridgewood Industrial Park,

Uckfield, East Sussex,

TN22 5QE England

Tel: +44 (0) 1825 749494

www.naval-military-press.com

www.nmarchive.com

This diary has been reprinted in facsimile from the original. Any imperfections are inevitably reproduced and the quality may fall short of modern type and cartographic standards.

© Crown Copyright
Images reproduced by permission of The National Archives, London, England, 2015.

Contents

Document type	Place/Title	Date From	Date To
Heading	WO95/2787/4 254 Machine Gun Company		
Heading	49th Division 254th Machine Gun Coy. Nov 1917-Mar 1918		
Heading	War Diary Of 254 Machine Gun Company No. 1 Nov 1917		
War Diary	Le Havre	15/11/1917	16/11/1917
War Diary	Ouderdom	17/11/1917	25/11/1917
War Diary	Montreal Camp	26/11/1917	30/11/1917
Heading	War Diary Of 254 Mach Gun Coy For December 1917 Vol 2		
War Diary	Montreal Camp H 19.b 40.60 Sheet 28	01/12/1917	05/12/1917
War Diary	H.18.c 20.30. Sheet 28	06/12/1917	31/12/1917
Operation(al) Order(s)	254th M.G. Coy Operation Order No. 1 Ref Map Sheet 28 1/40,000	04/12/1917	04/12/1917
Operation(al) Order(s)	254th Machine Gun Company Operation Order No. 2	07/12/1917	07/12/1917
Miscellaneous	A Form Messages And Signals		
Operation(al) Order(s)	254th Machine Gun Company Operation Order No. 3	08/12/1917	08/12/1917
Operation(al) Order(s)	254th Machine Gun Company Operation Order No. 4	09/12/1917	09/12/1917
Operation(al) Order(s)	254th Machine Gun Company Operation Order No. 5	11/12/1917	11/12/1917
Operation(al) Order(s)	254th Machine Gun Company Operation Order No. 6	12/12/1917	12/12/1917
Miscellaneous	W.X.Y.Z. Sections. D.M.G.O.	12/12/1917	12/12/1917
Operation(al) Order(s)	254th Machine Gun Company Operation Order No. 7	13/12/1917	13/12/1917
Miscellaneous	A Form Messages And Signals		
Miscellaneous	Y. Section Z. Section	15/12/1917	15/12/1917
Operation(al) Order(s)	254th Machine Gun Company Operation Order No. 8	16/12/1917	16/12/1917
Operation(al) Order(s)	254th Machine Gun Company Operation Order No. 9	18/12/1917	18/12/1917
Operation(al) Order(s)	254th Machine Gun Company Operation Order No. 10	20/12/1917	20/12/1917
Operation(al) Order(s)	254th Machine Gun Company Operation Order No. 11	22/12/1917	22/12/1917
Operation(al) Order(s)	254th Machine Gun Company Operation Order No. 12	24/12/1917	24/12/1917
Operation(al) Order(s)	254th Machine Gun Company Operation Order No. 13	26/12/1917	26/12/1917
Operation(al) Order(s)	254th Machine Gun Company Operation Order No. 14	27/12/1917	27/12/1917
Heading	War Diary Of 254th Machine Gun Company For January 1918 Vol 4		
War Diary	H.18.c 20.30. Sheet 28	01/01/1918	13/01/1918
War Diary	Caestre	14/01/1918	31/01/1918
Operation(al) Order(s)	254th Machine Gun Company Operation Order No. 15	01/01/1918	01/01/1918
Operation(al) Order(s)	254th Machine Gun Company Operation Order No. 16	02/01/1918	02/01/1918
Operation(al) Order(s)	254th Machine Gun Company Operation Order No. 17	05/01/1918	05/01/1918
Operation(al) Order(s)	254th Machine Gun Company Operation Order No. 18	07/01/1918	07/01/1918
Operation(al) Order(s)	254th Machine Gun Company Operation Order No. 19	11/01/1918	11/01/1918
Miscellaneous	Training Programme For The Week Ending 19th January 1918	19/01/1918	19/01/1918
Miscellaneous	Training Programme For The Week Ending 26th January 1918	26/01/1918	26/01/1918
Miscellaneous	Training Programme For The Week Ending 2nd February 1918	02/02/1918	02/02/1918
Heading	War Diary Of The 254th Machine Gun Company For February 1918 Vol 5		
War Diary	Caestre	01/02/1918	02/02/1918
War Diary	W.2.c.8.1	03/02/1918	21/02/1918

War Diary	I.8.d.6.6	22/02/1918	28/02/1918
War Diary	Caestre W.2.c.8.1	28/01/1918	11/02/1918
War Diary	30 Fde Ranger At 10.7a1.7	12/02/1918	16/02/1918
War Diary	Caestre W.2.c.8.1	18/02/1918	18/02/1918
War Diary	30 Yards Range At W.7.a.1.7	19/02/1918	23/02/1918
Operation(al) Order(s)	254th Machine Gun Company Operation Order No. 20	21/02/1918	21/02/1918
Operation(al) Order(s)	254th Machine Gun Company Operation Order No. 21		

wo/45/278714

254 Medline Cup Company.

49TH DIVISION

254TH MACHINE GUN COY.

NOV 1917-MAR 1918

Ref. C2g.

Vol I

War Diary.
of
254 Machine Gun Company

No. 1.

Nov 1917

Army Form C. 2118.

WAR DIARY
INTELLIGENCE SUMMARY — 254 Machine Gun Coy.
(Erase heading not required.)

Instructions regarding War Diaries and Intelligence Summaries are contained in F.S. Regs., Part II. and the Staff Manual respectively. Title pages will be prepared in manuscript.

Place	Date	Hour	Summary of Events and Information	Remarks and references to Appendices
Le Havre	15/11/17		Arrived from Southampton. Marched to No. 2 Rest Camp. SAN VIC.	
"	15.11.17		Equipping for the Line.	
"	16.11.17		Entrained at GARE DES MARCHADISES.	
Ouderdom	17.11.17		Detrained & marched to No. 11 Camp G.35.c.06 (Sheet 28)	
"	18.11.17		} Training and Equipping	
"	19.11.17			
"	20.11.17			
"	21.11.17		Route March.	
"	22.11.17		Training & Equipping. Orders received from 49th Div. not to move to Halifax Area on 26th but not. C.O. & 2nd in Command proceeded to Halifax Area and arranged with Commandant to move to Montreal Camp.	
"	23.11.17			
"	24.11.17			
"	25.11.17			
Montreal Camp	26.11.17		Orders received from 49th Div. Ga 649 of 25th to attach 30 men for instructional purposes to each of the 147th and 148th M.G.Coys; these men to report on the 26.11.17. Moved to Montreal Camp. Halifax Area H 19 b 40.60. (Sheet 28.) Reported move complete to 49th Div. by 3.10 p.m. "W" Section detailed to be attached to the 147th M.G. Coy and "X" Section to the 148th M.G. Coy. Moved off at 4.0 p.m. to report to their respective Coys. The Divisional Gas N.B.O. inspected the Box respirators of the Company. Training continued with "Y" and "Z" Sections	
"	27.11.17		During the period 15.11.17 to the 27.11.17 the casualties have been NIL.	
"	28.11.17		Cleaning Camp and drainage with "Y" and "Z" Sections remaining at duty.	
"	29.11.17		"W" and "X" Sections still under instruction in the Line. Training of "Y" and "Z" Sections continued. Casualties 1 O.R. wounded, including one. Casualties NIL.	
"	30.11.17			

J.R. Hoskins, Major
O.C. 254. M.G. Coy.

Secret

War Diary No 2

of

254 Mach Gun Coy

for

December 1917

Page 1.

Army Form C. 2118.

WAR DIARY

~~INTELLIGENCE SUMMARY.~~

(Erase heading not required.)

254th Machine Gun Company

Instructions regarding War Diaries and Intelligence Summaries are contained in F. S. Regs., Part II. and the Staff Manual respectively. Title pages will be prepared in manuscript.

Place	Date	Hour	Summary of Events and Information	Remarks and references to Appendices
MONTREAL CAMP. H.19.b.40.60. Sheet 28.	1.12.17.		Received D.M.G.O. 177. "W" and "X" Sections 'Machinement to cease on 3rd inst. and return to Helgro.	
	2.12.17		Received Warning order from D.M.G.O. 8 guns to be prepared to proceed to trenches to occupy "A" Battery (6 guns) and positions 9 and 10. on or after the 5th inst. Officers to reconnoitre line on 4th inst. Casualties NIL.	
"	3.12.17		Received 49th Div: Operation Order No 140. Relief to take place on morning of 5th. "W" and "X" Sections in line under instruction. "Y" and "Z" training. Casualties NIL. "W" and "X" Sections in line under instruction. "Y" and "Z" training. Received orders from D.M.G.O. to relieve "A" Battery (6 guns) and 9 and 10. positions (2 guns) occupied by 147th M.G. Coy. on morning of 5th inst. Relief to be complete by 9.0. a.m. "W" Section rejoined from the line. Casualties NIL.	
"	4.12.17		"X" Section reported from the line. Transport inspected by O.C. 49th Divisional Train. Section Officers reconnoitred the line. WIND DANGEROUS. Casualties NIL.	(1)
"	5.12.17		Relief complete 8.25 a.m. Company disposed "Z" Section near 2 guns "Y" Section "A" Battery. T.H.C. 00.40. No 9 position J4.b. 40.20. and No 10 position D.28.c.85.15. 2 guns "W" Section. Remainder in Reserve at Hdqrs. Casualties NIL.	
H.18.c.20.30. Sheet 28.	6.12.17.		Moved to CANAL AREA. Hdgs established H.18.c. 20.30. Casualties NIL.	(2)
"	7.12.17.		Reserve Sections improving Camp. Issued Operation Order No.2. Instruction Relief Casualties NIL.	(3)
"	8.12.17.		Reserve Sections improving Camp. Issued Amendment to Operation Order No.2. Guides to be at BIRR CROSS ROADS at 7 a.m. instead of 7 a.m. on 9th inst. D.M.G.C. called at Hdqrs and gave following instructions. "Owing to change in Divisional boundary "A" Battery position was to be handed over to the N.Z. Division and that on the morning of the 9th "A" Battery with Section Officer into Reserve. He will reconnoitre a new position for his Battery with Section Officer on morning of 9th inst. He also gave instructions that the new battery would consist of 4 guns, and we were to take over two new positions Nos 11. and 12 from the 148th M.G. Coy. on the morning of the 9th inst. Joined Operation Order No.3 dealing with above. Casualties NIL.	
"	9.12.17.		Relief of Nos 11 and 12 positions by "W" Section complete by 9.a.m. Withdrawal of "A" Battery complete	(4)

[signature] Major
Commanding 254 M.G. Coy.

Page 2.

Army Form C. 2118.

WAR DIARY
INTELLIGENCE SUMMARY.
(Erase heading not required.)

257th Machine Gun Company

Instructions regarding War Diaries and Intelligence Summaries are contained in F. S. Regs., Part II. and the Staff Manual respectively. Title pages will be prepared in manuscript.

Place	Date	Hour	Summary of Events and Information	Remarks and references to Appendices
H18C 20.30. Sheet 28.	9.12.17.		without hitch. Received instructions from D.M.G.O. giving new position of "A" Battery T3 b 20.25. and that work on same was to be commenced at once, and it was to be ready to answer S.O.S. calls on the night of the 12/13 inst. Issued Operation Order No.4. to "X" Section to commence this work. Casualties NIL.	(5)
"	10.12.17.		Work on new Battery position for "A" Battery commenced. Good progress made. Received instructions from D.M.G.O. that line "A" Battery to be ready for S.O.S calls from 12/13 to 13/14. Disposition of Company "W" Section in the line holding Nos 9.10.11. and 12 positions. "X" Section working party for "A" Battery. "Y" and "Z" Sections in Reserve. Casualties NIL.	
"	11.12.17.		Work on new Battery position continued by "X" Section. Dugout nearly completed. Issued Operation Order No.5. detailing "X" Section to occupy "A" Battery and to be ready to answer S.O.S. by 7.30.p.m on the 12th inst. (Casualties NIL).	(6)
"	12.12.17.		"X" Section proceeded to line and manned "A" Battery. Readiness to answer S.O.S. calls was wired by O.C. "A" Battery to D.M.G.O. by 7.30.p.m. Issued Operation Order No.6 "Y" Section to relieve "W" Section on 13th inst. Issued S.C.H. 122. No 9.10.11. and 12. guns to co-operate in Divisional Harassing Fire Scheme. Casualties NIL.	(7)
"	13.12.17.		Relief of "W" Section by "Y" Section complete by 9.a.m. Issued Operation Order No.7. "Z" Section to relieve "X" Section on the 15th inst. Casualties NIL.	(8)
"	14.12.17.		C.O. went round the line with the Divisional Commander. Fairly quiet day. Harassing fire commenced at 12. noon. Targets issued by 148th Infantry Brigade. Casualties NIL.	(9)
"	15.12.17.		Relief of "A" Battery by "Z" Section complete by 9.0.a.m. Issued S.C.H. 134. new S.O.S. signal to come into force on the 19th inst. Issued S.C.H. 135. re a test S.O.S. to be fired by the 148th Infantry Brigade. Harassing fire continued.	(10) (11)
"	16.12.17.		Work on emplacements and dug-outs continued. "Y" Section fired 3000 rounds on selected targets in co-operation with Divisional Harassing fire scheme. An extraordinary shell was observed at "A" Battery, which on detonation emitted a flare resembling a Verey light. It was believed to be a ranging shell. Desultory shelling throughout the day with 5.9's and 4.2's. Casualties NIL.	
"	17.12.17.		"W" Section relieved "Y" Section in Nos 9.10.11. and 12. positions. 1750 Rounds were fired on selected targets during the day and night of 17/18th. Casualties NIL.	(12)

Continued on .... A M.G. Coy.

Page 3.

Army Form C. 2118.

WAR DIARY

INTELLIGENCE SUMMARY. 25th Machine Gun Company

(Erase heading not required.)

Instructions regarding War Diaries and Intelligence Summaries are contained in F.S. Regs., Part II. and the Staff Manual respectively. Title pages will be prepared in manuscript.

Place	Date	Hour	Summary of Events and Information	Remarks and references to Appendices
H.18.c. 20.90. Sheet 28.	18.12.17		No.10 Gun emplacement received a direct hit. Casualties NIL. Work on "P" Battery continued. Vicinity of Battery lightly shelled. Casualties NIL.	
"	19.12.17		"X" Section relieved "Z" Section at "P" Battery. 1000 Rounds fired in irregular bursts on targets chosen to co-operate with the scheme of Harassing Fire. Casualties NIL.	(13)
"	20.12.17		Severe frost made work difficult on account of the hardness of the ground. This also necessitated the guns being fired intermittently in order to keep them in action. S.C.H. 173 re Defensive Measures against Mustard gas issued to Sections.	No.9 O'Connell A.gun recommended this No. 91-92 and 93 guns
"	21.12.17		"Y" Section relieved "W" Section. Webb in forward area frozen, so that water for the Sections had to be sent to Sections in the line from Company H'qrs. Casualties 1 O.R. wounded.	(14)
"	22.12.17		Section reports about this date indicate that enemy shelling has gradually been decreasing in intensity. At the same time however, it has become more accurate, especially on junctions of tracks and Battery positions. Casualties NIL.	(15)
"	23.12.17		"Z" Section relieved "X" Section at "P" Battery. C.O. went to Divisional H'qrs re D.W.G.O. 20.tem. Weather this extremely cold but dry.	
"	24.12.17		28,000 Rounds S.P.B drawn from GARTER POINT DUMP for "P" Battery. A very quiet day. Casualties NIL.	(16)
"	25.12.17		Christmas Day. After a light snow, snow fell throughout the day. "W" Section relieved "Y" Section in Nos. 90, 91, 92 and 93 positions.	
"	26.12.17		S.O.S. observed on the right flank, but no action was taken on our Divisional front. Casualties NIL.	
"	27.12.17		S.O.S. signals observed on Divisional Front at 7.47.p.m. All guns opened rapid fire on S.O.S. lines. A total of 23,600 rounds was fired by the 8 guns of the Company. (Advanced Guns and "P" Battery). No attack developed. Casualties NIL. The usual Harassing fire continued by Nos. 90, 91, 92 and 93 guns. WATTLE DUMP. The enemy was for some reason, was submitted to a concentration shoot about 7 a.m. Several casualties occurred, but a party of men from the Company succeeded in avoiding it by making a detour. This is frequently possible when the enemy indulges in shelling of this kind. Casualties NIL.	
"	28.12.17		"X" Section relieved "Z" Section at "P" Battery. Hostile Artillery activity normal. 5000 Rounds	(17)

Page 4.

Army Form C. 2118.

WAR DIARY

~~INTELLIGENCE SUMMARY~~

254. Machine Gun Company.

(Erase heading not required.)

Place	Date	Hour	Summary of Events and Information	Remarks and references to Appendices
H.18.C.20.30 Sheet 28.	28.12.17		Fired by advanced guns on indirect targets. Casualties NIL.	
	29.12.17		"Y" Section relieved "W" Section. Lt. R.D. ELLIS proceeded to WISQUES for a course at Second Army School. Quiet day in the line.	
	30.12.17		Conditions in the line normal. Hostile Artillery unusually quiet. Draft of 5 O.R's received from Base. Casualties NIL.	
	31.12.17		S.O.S. observed on the left flank at 6.8. a.m. but was not repeated on Divisional Front. Slight thaw rendered more work on gun positions again possible. For harassing fire, advanced guns expended 2450. rounds S.A.A. Casualties NIL.	

J. Rushton Major.
Commanding 254 M.G. Coy.

254th M.G. Coy.　　　①　　　Copy No 7
Operation Order No 1　　　　　　Dec 4th 1917.
Ref Map Sheet 28. 1/40.000.

1. The Company will take over A. Battery. J 4 c 00.40.
No 9 gun position J 4 b 35.20. and No 10 gun
position D 28. c 85.15. from the 147th M.G. Coy on
the 5th inst.

2. A Battery consisting of 6 guns will be composed as
follows:-
　　　4 guns Z Section
　　　2 guns Y Section.
Battery Commander Lt. H. B. Churchill, with 2nd
in Command Lt. J. B. Brown.
Battery Hdqrs:- J 4 c 00. 40.
(a) Guides will be at Hdqrs 147th M.G. Coy H 18. c 20.20.
at 2.0. a.m. on the 5th inst.
(b) Trench Stores & S.A.A. will be taken over and
receipts given and copies sent to Hdqrs.
(c) Team Strengths will be 4 men per gun.
(d) Battery Maps & gun charts will be taken over
and receipts given.

3. No 9 & 10 gun positions will be occupied by W. Section.
(a) Guides will be at Hdqrs 147th M.G. Coy H 18. c 20.20.
at 2.0. a.m. on the 5th inst.
(b) Trench Stores & S. A.A. will be taken over and
receipts given, and copies sent to Hdqrs.
(c) Team strengths will be 4 men per gun.

4. Company Hdqrs will not move from Montreal
Camp at present

5. Relief to be complete by 9.0. a.m 5th inst & reported
to D.M.G.O. 49th Div. by code word HOOGE.

Copy No 1.　　W. Section
Copy No 2　　X. Section
Copy No 3　　Y. Section　　　　　Chas. Haskins
Copy No 4　　Z. Section　　　　　　　　　Major.
Copy No 5　　147th M.G. Coy.　　O.C. 254. M.G. Coy.
Copy No 6　　D.M.G.O. 49th Div.
　　Issued at 6.0 p.m.

254th Machine Gun Company.

Operation Order No 2.

SECRET.   Copy No 6

Reference - Map. Sheet 28. 1/40.000.

1. The following Inter Section Reliefs will take place on the morning of the 9th inst.

   (a) A. Battery will be relieved by:-

       4 guns X. Section.
       2 guns Y. Section.

   Battery Commander Lieut. A.O. Rees.
   2nd in Command Lieut. A.K. Steel.

   (b) Nos 9 and 10 guns will be relieved by W. Section.

   Commander Lieut. R.D. Ellis. M.C.

   Guides. 3 for A Battery, and one for 9 and 10 guns will be at BIRR CROSS ROADS at 4.0. a.m. on the 9th inst.

2. Trench Stores, S.A.A. Battery maps, Range charts and Orders will be handed over, and receipts taken; Copies to be sent at first opportunity to Hdqrs.

3. Acknowledge.

          S. Jas. Huskins
          Major.
          O.C. 254. M.G. Company.

Copy No 1 to W Section.
      2 " X Section.
      3 " Y. Section.
      4 " Z. Section.
      5 " D.M.G.O 49th Division for information

7/12/17

"A" Form
MESSAGES AND SIGNALS.
Army Form C. 2121
(In pads of 100.)
No. of Message..........

SECRET.

TO: W. X. Y. Z Sections
D.M.G.O. 49th Div for information

Sender's Number: SCH 97.
Day of Month: 8
In reply to Number:
AAA

Ref	O.O.	No 2	of
7th inst	AAA	Guides	will
be	at	BIRK	CROSS
ROADS	at	7 A.M.	9th inst
instead	of	4 A.M.	

From 254th M.G. Coy.
Place
Time 11.30 A.M.

Jas. Haskins Major

254th Machine Gun Company.
Operation Order No 3.

SECRET   Copy No 6

Reference Map. Sheet 28. 1/40,000.
                                          Dec 8th 1917

1. Operation Order No 2 of 7th inst is cancelled.

2. W Section on the morning of the 9th inst will relieve two guns of the 148th Machine Gun Coy.
   No 11 position D 28 c 45. 50.
   No 12 position D 28 c 30. 65.

   Guides for these positions will be at No 10 gun position at 8.0 a.m. 9th inst.

   Belt boxes will be taken over from Y Section at A Battery.

   Lt BURNIE will remain in Command of Nos 9. 10. 11. and 12. guns. He will arrange internal relief of Nos 9 and 10 positions. He will arrange to have a guide at A Battery Hdqrs at 6.30 a.m. to guide his incoming teams to No 10 position.

3. At 7.0 a.m. on the 9th inst A Battery will withdraw and return to depôt H 18. c 20. 30.

   (a) O.C. A Battery will obtain a receipt for Belt boxes handed to W Section. Remaining Belt boxes will be stacked in Pill box and left under a guard of two men.

   (b) Limber will be at BIRR CROSS ROADS at 7 a.m.

   (c) O.C. A Battery will arrange to have 2 guides at BIRR CROSS ROADS at 4.30 a.m. on the 9th inst. to guide W. Section to A Battery Hdqrs.

4. Lt A.K. STEEL and Lt R.D. ELLIS will arrange to meet D.M.G.O. 49th Division at A Battery Hdqrs at 8.30. a.m. on the 9th inst to reconnoitre a new position for A Battery.

Copy No 1. W. Section
       2. X Section
       3. Y Section
       4. Z Section
       5. D.M.G.O. for reference.

                                    Major.
                                O.C. 254 M.G.Coy.

254th Machine Gun Company.

Operation Order No. 4.

<u>SECRET.</u>

X. Section.

Dec 9th 1917.

1. The new position for A Battery which was selected by the D.M.G.O. 49th Division today, and as shown to you is near HELLES J.3.b.20.25 (exact locality requires further verification by resection)

2. A Battery will now consist of four guns, and will be in readiness to answer S.O.S calls at midnight on the 12th inst.

3. Accommodation for the teams i.e. 4 men per gun, 1 Sergeant and 1 Corporal, will be constructed on the West side of Pill boxes now occupied by R.A.M.C. and Divisional Signal Test Station.

4. Material can be obtained from YORKSHIRE DUMP J.&.3.c.30.80.
The shelters will be constructed with segments of corrugated iron.

5. The Emplacements for the time being will consist of a platform of 2 Sandbags thick, with T bases; These will be salved from old A Battery position.

6. Accommodation for one Officer is being arranged for in the PILL BOX occupied by the Divisional Signal Test Station.

7. As soon as the position is found by resection, the position of barrage will be worked out and handed to you.

8. You will proceed to the Line at 5.0.a.m with your Section to commence the work.

J. Geo. Haskin Major
O.C. 254 M.G. Coy.

254th Machine Gun Company.
Operation Order No. 5.

SECRET.

Copy No. 6
December 11th 1917.

Reference Map Sheet 28 1/40.000.

1. X Section will occupy A Battery (4 guns) Map reference of left hand gun J 3 b 25.15.
    Commander LT. A.K. STEEL.
    (a) O.C. Y. Section will detail 10 men to report to O.C. X. Section as carrying party on the 12th at 5.0. a.m. These men to return to Hdqrs on completion of journey.

2. A. Battery will be ready to open fire on S.O.S. calls by 4.30. p.m. on the 12th inst.

3. Battery Map with calculations, also Trajectory chart is attached. Standing Orders have been issued to all concerned.

4. Arrangements will be made as soon as possible to form a Dump of S.A.A. in a convenient position. Establishment of dump to be 40.000 rounds.

5. Battery ready in position will be wired to D.M.G.O. Code word GLOY.

6. Acknowledge.

Issued at 9.0. p.m.
Copy No 1. W. Section.
  2 X   "   *
  3 Y   "   *
  4. DMGO. 49th Div *
  5. War Diary.
  6. Spare.

S. Jas. Hastings. Major.
Commanding 254. M.G. Coy.

*. With Map & Chart.

254 Machine Gun Company
Operation Order No 6

SECRET.   Copy No. 6
                                              12th December 1917.

1. Y Section will relieve W Section in Nos. 9, 10, 11 and 12 positions on the morning of the 13th inst.
    (a) Y Section will leave Headquarters at 5.0 a.m.
    (b) Belt boxes and Tripods will be handed over, and receipts given.
    (c) Range and barrage charts will be carefully handed over.
    (d) A Limber will be at BIRR. CROSS ROADS at 10.30. a.m. to fetch out W. Sections' guns.
2. Lt. A.O. REES will be in command of Nos. 9, 10, 11 and 12 positions.
3. Relief complete will be reported to Hdqrs by wire: Code word DEFENDU.
4. W and Y Sections to acknowledge.

                                    B. Huskins, Major.
                                    Commanding 254. M.G.Coy.

Issued at 9.0 p.m.

  Copy No. 1 to W. Section.
       2 "   Y Section.
       3 "   X   ⎫
       4 "   Z   ⎬
       5 "   D.M.G.O. ⎭ for information.
       6 "   War Diary.
       7 "   Spare.

SECRET.
W. X. Y. Z. Sections.   D.M.G.O.

S.C.H. 122.   A.A.A.   December 12th 1917.

1. Nos 9. 10. 11 and 12 guns will cooperate in the Divisional Harassing fire scheme. The Officer commanding these guns will arrange each day for the nights shoot with the Officer commanding the Right Brigade M.G. Company. These guns will fire on a special Sector known as LANE "F".

2. A Battery in order to ensure that its guns are timed, will fire short bursts at extreme Range every day during the periods of Darkness.

3. Addressed W. X. Y. Z. Sections repeated D.M.G.O. for information.

4. Acknowledge.

Has Hastin Major.
Commanding 254. M.G.Coy.

254 Machine Gun Company.
Operation Order No 7.

SECRET.   Copy No 6
Reference. Map Sheet 28 1/40,000.   December 13th 1917.

1. Z Section will relieve X Section in A Battery position on the morning of the 15th inst.
   (a) Battery Commander. Lt. H. B. CHURCHILL.
   (b) Z. Section will leave Hdqrs at 5.30. a.m.
   (c) X Section will provide two guides to be at BIRR CROSS ROAD at 7.0. a.m.
2. Tripods and belt boxes will be handed over.
3. O.C. X Section will hand over Scheme of work for the improvement of the position.
4. Relief complete will be reported by wire to Hdqrs. Code word "POOCHE".
5. X and Z Sections to acknowledge.

                              J. Bas. Haslam Major.
Issued at 10.0. p.m.   Commanding 254. M.G. Coy.

        Copy No 1 to X. Section.
             2 „ Z. Section.
             3 „ W. Section.
             4 „ Y. Section.   ⎫
             5 „ D.M.G.O. 49th Div ⎬ for information
             6 „ War Diary.   ⎭
             7   Spare.

"A" Form
MESSAGES AND SIGNALS.

Army Form C. 2121
(in pads of 100).

SECRET

TO: W.X.Y.Z. Section

Sender's Number	Day of Month	In reply to Number	AAA
S.C.H.134	15		

Commencing from NOON on 19th December the S.O.S. Signal throughout the Army will be a Rifle Grenade Signal bursting into 2 Red 2 White stars simultaneously AAA Commencing at the same time and date the Enemies barrage Signal will be a light changing from WHITE to GREEN AAA Acknowledge

From 254th M.G. Company
Place
Time

(Z) S. Bas. Haskins Major

SECRET   December 15th 1917.

Y. Section.
Z.   "

1. The method of passing on S.O.S. Signals will be tested by the 148th Infantry Brigade on the 16th inst between "Stand to" at Dawn and "Stand to" at Sunset.

2. The Signal for "TEST" will be three Very Lights fired from the front line, and passed on by relay stations to Coy Hdqrs, Bn. Hdqrs, M.G. Barrage Batteries, and Bn. Hdqrs of Support Bn.
   Warning will also be passed on by Wireless, Power Buzzer, Telegraph and visual by sending the word "TEST".

3. The Artillery on receipt will fire one round on S.O.S. lines. A Battery will fire a short burst with <u>one gun</u>: Nos 9. 10. 11 and 12 guns will fire a short burst on S.O.S. lines.

4. Time to be taken from first signal seen to firing of gun, and also of receipt of the message by other means.

5. A report on the result of this test will be sent to Hdqrs as soon as possible.

6. Watches will be synchronised by signals.

                                                      [signature] Major

Issued at 2.0 p.m.
    S.C.H. 135

254th Machine Gun Company.
Operation Order No. 8.

Ref Map. Sheet 28. 1/40.000.　　　　Copy No. 7.

1. W. Section will relieve Y Section in Nos 9. 10. 11. and 12 positions on the morning of the 17th.
   (a) Guide will be at WATTLE DUMP at 7.0.a.m.
   (b) W. Section will leave Hdqrs at 5.0.a.m.
   (c) Belt boxes and Tripods will be handed over.
   (d) Limber will be at BIRR CROSS ROADS at 10.30.a.m to bring out Y. Section's guns.

2. Programme of Harassing fire will be carefully explained, and continued by W. Section in Liaison with the 148th M.G. Company.

3. Relief complete will be reported to Hdqrs by wire by code word "POO OP".

4. W. and Y. Sections to acknowledge.

Issued at 7.0.p.m.

　　　　　　　　　　　　　Geo. Haskins Major
　　　　　　　　　　　　Commanding 254. M.G.Coy.

Copy No 1 to W. Section.
　　　2 " Y. Section.
　　　3 " X Section.
　　　4 " Z Section.
　　　5 " D.M.G.O. 49th Div. } for information.
　　　6 " 148. Inf Bde.
　　　7 " War Diary.
　　　8 " Spare.

254th Machine Gun Company.
Operation Order No. 9.

SECRET Copy No. 7

Ref. Map. Sheet 28 1/40.000.   December 18th 1917.

1. "X" Section will relieve "Z" Section in "A" Battery position on the morning of the 19th inst.
   (a) Battery Commander Lt. R.D. ELLIS. M.C.
   (b) "X" Section will leave Hdqrs at 5.30. a.m.

2. Tripods and 28 belt boxes will be handed over. "Z" Section will bring out 28 belts in boxes. "X" Section will carry in 28 belts in boxes.

3. O.C. "Z" Section will hand over all battery charts, maps, and the scheme of work for the improvement of the position.

4. Relief complete will be reported by wire to Hdqrs by the code word. "DINDE".

5. "X" and "Z" Sections to acknowledge.

Issued at 3.0.p.m.

[signature] Major.
Commanding 254. M.G.Coy.

Copy No. 1 to X. Section.
     2 " Z. Section.
     3. W. Section
     4. Y. Section.
     5. D.M.G.O. 49th Div. } for information.
     6. 148th Inf Bgde. }
     7. War Diary.
     8. Spare.

254th Machine Gun Company.
Operation Order No 10.

SECRET
Copy No ...7...
December 20th 1917.

Ref. Map Sheet 28. 1/40.000

1. "Y" Section will relieve "W" Section in Nos. 90. 91. 92. and 93. positions on the morning of the 21st inst.
   (a) Y Section will leave Headquarters at 5.30. a.m.
   (b) Lt. J.B. BROWN will relieve Lt. J.B. BURNIE.

2. Tripods and belt boxes will be handed over.

3. O.C. "W" Section will hand over all maps, standing Orders, and scheme of harassing fire.

4. Relief complete will be wired to Hdqrs, code word "BARKSTON".

5. "W" and "Y" Sections to acknowledge.

Issued at 7.0. p.m.

           S.C. Geo. Haskins Major.
           Commanding 254. M.G. Coy.

Copy No 1 to "W" Section
"   " 2 " "Y" Section
"   " 3 " "X" "
"   " 4 " "Z" "
"   " 5 " D.M.G.O. 19th Div. } for information
"   " 6 " 148th Inf. Bgde.   }
"   " 7 " War Diary.
"   " 8 " Spare.

254th Machine Gun Company.
Operation Order No 11.

SECRET Copy No. 7

Ref. Map Sheet 28. 1/40.000. December 22nd 1917.

1. "Z" Section will relieve "X" Section at "A" BATTERY position on the morning of the 23rd inst.
   (a) Battery Commander Lt. H.B. CHURCHILL.
   (b) "Z" Section will leave Coy. Hdqrs. at 5.30.a.m.

2. Tripods and 28 Belt boxes will be handed over.
   "Z" Section will carry in 28 Belt boxes.
   "X" Section will bring out 28 Belt boxes.

3. O.C. "X" Section will hand over all Maps, Battery Charts, and Standing Orders.

4. Relief complete will be wired to Company Hdqrs. Code word "TOUCHEZ".

5. "X" and "Z" Sections to acknowledge.

Issued at 9.0.a.m.

J. Chas. Hastin, Major.
Commanding 254. M.G. Coy.

Copy No. 1 to "X" Section.
"   "   2 . "Z" Section
"   "   3 . "W" Section.
"   "   4 . "Y" Section.
"   "   5 . D.M.G.O. 49th Div. } for information.
"   "   6 . 148th Inf. Bgde.   }
"   "   7 . War Diary.
"   "   8   Spare.

254th Machine Gun Company.
Operation Order No 12.

SECRET Copy. No 7.

Ref. Map Sheet 28 1/40.000.   December 24th 1917.

1. "W" Section will relieve "Y" Section in Nos. 90. 91. 92. and 93. positions on the morning of the 25th inst.
   (a) "W" Section will leave Hdqrs at 5.30.a.m.
   (b) Lt. H. R. HESKETH will relieve Lt. J.B. BROWN.

2. Tripods & belt boxes will be handed over.

3. Maps, Standing Orders, Scheme of harassing fire, and Trench Stores will be handed over. Receipts will be given & copies sent to Hdqrs.

4. Relief complete will be wired to Hdqrs. Code word "YATES."

5. "W" and "Y" Sections to acknowledge.

Issued at 6.0.p.m.

                         [signature] Major.
                 Commanding 254. M.G. Coy.

Copy No 1. to "W" Section.
" " 2 " "Y" "
" " 3 " "X" "
" " 4 " "Z" " } for information.
" " 5 " D.M.G.O. 49th Div.
" " 6 " 147th Inf Bgde.
" " 7 " War Diary
" " 8 " Spare.

254th Machine Gun Company
Operation Order No. 13.

SECRET.

Copy No 7.

Ref. Map Sheet 28. 1/40.000.   December 26th 1917.

1. "X" Section will relieve "Z" Section at "H" Battery position on the morning of the 28th inst.
   (a) Battery Commander Lt. A.K. STEEL.
   (b) "X" Section will leave Coy. Hdqrs at 5.30. a.m.

2. Tripods and 28 belt boxes will be handed over. "X" Section will take in 28 belt boxes. "Z" Section will bring out 28 belt boxes.

3. O.C. "Z" Section will hand over to O.C. "X" Section all maps, Battery Charts, Standing orders, and Trench stores. Receipts will be sent to Hdqrs.

4. Relief complete will be wired to Hdqrs. Code word "ZAIDA".

5. "X" and "Z" Sections to acknowledge.

Issued at 7.30. p.m.

W. Inskip Capt. Major.
Commanding 254. M.G. Coy.

Copy No 1. to "X" Section
  "   " 2. " "Z"   "
  "   " 3. " "W"   "
  "   " 4. " "Y"   "
  "   " 5. " D.M.G.O. 49th Div. ⎫
  "   " 6. " 147th Inf Bde.   ⎬ for information.
  "   " 7. " War Diary   ⎭
  "   " 8. " Spare.

254th Machine Gun Company.
Operation Order No. 14.

SECRET   Copy No. 7.

Ref. Map Sheet 28. 1/40.000.   December 27th 1917.

1. "Y" Section will relieve "W" Section in Nos. 90. 91. 92. and 93 gun positions on the morning of the 29th inst.
   (a) "Y" Section will leave Hdqrs at 5.30. a.m.
   (b) Lt. A.O. REES will relieve Lt. H.R. HESKETH.

2. Tripods and belt boxes will be handed over.

3. O.C. "W" Section will hand over to O.C. "Y" Section, all Maps, Standing Orders, Scheme of harassing fire, and Trench Stores. Receipts to be sent to Company Hdqrs.

4. Relief complete will be wired to Hdqrs. code word "PATUM".

5. "W" and "Y" Sections to acknowledge.

   Issued at 6.0. p.m.

                                    White Capt/Major.
                              Commanding 254. M.G. Coy.

Copy No. 1. to "Y" Section
  "   " 2. " "W"   "
  "   " 3. " "X"   "
  "   " 4. " "Z"   "
  "   " 5. " D.M.G.O. 49th Div. } for information.
  "   " 6. " 147th Inf. Bgde.   }
  "   " 7. War Diary
  "   " 8. Spare.

W 4

War Diary
of
254th Machine-Gun Company
for
January 1918.

Sheet. 1.

Army Form C. 2118.

WAR DIARY
INTELLIGENCE SUMMARY.
(Erase heading not required.)

254th Machine Gun Company

Instructions regarding War Diaries and Intelligence Summaries are contained in F. S. Regs., Part II. and the Staff Manual respectively. Title pages will be prepared in manuscript.

Place	Date	Hour	Summary of Events and Information	Remarks and references to Appendices
J.18.c 20.30.	1/1/18.		4000 Rds S.A.A. were fired by advanced guns on indirect targets. Shaken at "A".	
Sheet 28.			Battery normal. Work on mens' Dug-out completed. Slight shelling, many of the shells being "Duds". Casualties NIL.	
"	2.1.18.		"W" Section relieved "Y" Section in Nos. 90, 91, 92, and 93 Gun positions.	15.
			Exceptionally quiet during the day. Casualties NIL.	
			"Z" Section relieved "X" Section at "A" Battery.	16.
"	3.1.18.		Gas alarm at Section Headquarters of Advanced guns at 10.40.p.m. Lasted a few minutes. It originated in gas from shells in the vicinity of ZONNEBEKE. There was a certain amount of shrapnel and Machine Gun fire on Nos. 90 and 92 gun positions. Otherwise quiet day.	
"	4.1.18.		Hostile Artillery very active on squares J.3.a and J.3.b. Reconnoitred ground in front of advanced guns, and selected new positions for these guns in order to secure a better field of fire on wire entanglements of Reserve Line.	
"	5.1.18.		Ammunition supply made good from Dumps at GARTER POINT. Work on new emplacement for No.91 commenced, but progress poor on account of the frozen condition of the ground. Nos 92 and 93 guns were shelled, probably by gas.	

J.W. W---- ---- Major.
Commanding 254 M.G.Coy.

Sheet 2.

Army Form C. 2118.

WAR DIARY
INTELLIGENCE SUMMARY
254th Machine Gun Company.

(Erase heading not required.)

Place	Date	Hour	Summary of Events and Information	Remarks and references to Appendices
H.18.c.20.30. Sheet 28.	5.1.18		There was considerable movement above ground in the neighbouring Infantry post. At "A" Battery one gun was temporarily put out of action by a "shell" splinter perforating the barrel casing.	
"	6.1.18		Orders received to gradually reduce Harassing Fire, and finally to stop it altogether. "A" Battery heavily shelled. Two direct hits on men's Pill Box, 1 ammunition & front dumps fired. Twenty one belt boxes were destroyed or damaged by shell fire. Casualties Nil.	
"	7.1.18.		The usual trench routine undisturbed by hostile activity. Only a few rounds fired by the guns to prevent them from freezing.	
"	8.1.18.		"Y" Section relieved "W" Section at the advanced guns. "X" Section relieved "Z" Section at "A" Battery.	17 18
"	9.1.18.		New positions for No.9 Gun completed, but not occupied on account of the coming relief of the Company by the 202nd M.G. Company. Situation normal. The night was intensely cold, with strong rear wind. Great trouble was experienced in preventing the guns from freezing. Casualties Nil.	
"	10.1.18.		A number of gas shells fell near "A" Battery. On account of the weather only work on cleaning ammunition and belts was possible.	

J.W. Hutchins
Capt.
Comdg 254 M.G. Co.

Sheet 3.

Army Form C. 2118.

WAR DIARY
or
INTELLIGENCE SUMMARY.
(Erase heading not required.)

254th Machine Gun Company

Instructions regarding War Diaries and Intelligence Summaries are contained in F.S. Regs., Part II. and the Staff Manual respectively. Title pages will be prepared in manuscript.

Place	Date	Hour	Summary of Events and Information	Remarks and references to Appendices
P.18.C 20.30.	11.1.18.		A concentrated shoot by the enemy took place on the Pill Boxes at "P" Battery. One shell	
Sheet 28.			blew in Pill Southern Buttress of Mess Dug-out and turned Pat Belly. He was however only shaken. Two other men were sent to By. H.Qrs. with Shell shock. Otherwise there were no casualties.	19.
"	12.1.18		Met O.C. 202nd M.G.Coy: Arranged details of relief with him, and issued Operation Order No 19.	
"			Went round the line with O.C. 202nd M.G.Company immediately prior to relief. The relief was complete about 8.30. a.m.	
"	13.1.18		Handed over Camp at P.18.c.20.30. Sheet 28. to 202nd M.G.Company. Company embussed at BELGIAN CHATEAU, and debussed at CAESTRE. Move to CAESTRE was complete by 4.0.p.m.	
CAESTRE	14.1.18.		Cleaning and Re-equipping.	
"	15.1.18.		Cleaning guns and equipment	
"	16.1.18		Training as per programme I.	I
"	17-31. Jan 1918		Training as per programmes I, II and III.	II & III

S.W. Hutchins
Commanding 254 M.G. Coy.

254th Machine Gun Company.
Operation Order No. 15.

SECRET Copy No. 7.

Ref. Map. Sheet 28 1/40.000.   1st January 1918.

1. "W" Section will relieve "Y" Section in Nos. 90. 91. 92. and 93 gun positions on the morning of the 2nd inst.
   (a) "W" Section will leave Hdqrs at 6.30. a.m.
   (b) LT. J.B. BURNIE will relieve LT. A.O. REES.

2. Tripods and belt boxes will be handed over.

3. O.C. "Y" Section will hand over to O.C. "W" Section all Maps, Standing Orders, Scheme of Harassing fire, and Trench Stores. Copies of receipts to be sent to Company Headquarters.

4. Relief complete will be wired to Headquarters. Code word "INTACTO".

5. "W" and "Y" Sections to acknowledge.

Issued at 12. noon.

White Capt Major.
Commanding 254th M.G. Coy.

Copy No. 1 to "W" Section.
"   " 2 " "Y" Section.
"   " 3 " "X" Section.
"   " 4 " "Z" Section.   ⎫
"   " 5 " D.M.G.O. 49th Div. ⎬ for information.
"   " 6 " 147th Inf. Bgde.   ⎭
"   " 7 " War Diary.
"   " 8 " Spare.

254th Machine Gun Company.
Operation Order No. 16.

SECRET.   Copy No 7.

Ref Map. Sheet 28. 1/40.000.   2nd January 1918.

1. "Z" Section will relieve "X" Section at "A" Battery on the morning of the 3rd inst.
   (a) Battery Commander Lt. H. B. CHURCHILL.
   (b) "Z" Section will leave Hdqrs at 5.30. a.m.

2. Tripods and 28 belt boxes will be handed over. "Z" Section will take in 28 belt boxes. "X" Section will bring out 28 belt boxes.

3. O.C. "X" Section will hand over to O.C. "Z" Section all Maps, Battery chart, Standing orders, and Trench stores. Receipts will be sent to Hdqts.

4. Relief complete will be wired to Headquarters. Code word "MAFEESH".

5. "Z" and "X" Sections to acknowledge.

Issued at 11.30.a.m.

W. Nutie Capt. & Major
Commanding 254th M.G.Coy.

Copy No 1 to "Z" Section.
  "   " 2 " "X" Section.
  "   " 3 " "W" Section.
  "   " 4 " "Y" Section.   ⎫
  "   " 5 " D.M.G.O. 49th Div. ⎬ for information.
  "   " 6 " 147 Inf Bgde.   ⎭
  "   " 7 " War Diary.
  "   " 8 " Spare.

254th Machine Gun Company.
Operation Order No. 17.

SECRET.   Copy No. 7.

Ref Map. Sheet 28. 1/40.000.   5th January 1918.

1. "Y" Section will relieve "W" Section in Nos. 90. 91. 92 and 93 gun positions on the morning of the 7th inst.
   (a) "Y" Section will leave Hdqrs at 5. a.m.
   (b) Lt. J. B. BROWN will relieve Lt. J. B. BURNIE.

2. Tripods and belt boxes will be handed over.

3. O.C. "W" Section will hand over to O.C. "Y" Section all Maps, Standing Orders, Scheme of Harassing fire, and Trench Stores. Copies of receipts to be sent to Company Headquarters.

4. Relief complete will be wired to Headquarters. Code word "POPIN".

5. "Y" and "W" Sections to acknowledge.

Issued at 11. 30. a.m.

W Milne Capt Major.
Commanding 254th M.G. Coy.

Copy No. 1 to "Y" Section.
 "   " 2 - "W" Section.
 "   " 3 - "X" Section.   ⎫
 "   " 4 - "Z" Section.   ⎬ for information.
 "   " 5 - D.M.G.O. 49th Div.   ⎭
 "   " 6 - 146th Inf Bgde.
 "   " 7 - War Diary.
 "   " 8 - Spare.

254th Machine Gun Company.
Operation Order No. 18.

<u>SECRET</u> Copy No. 7

Ref Map. Sheet 28. 1/40.000.   7th January 1918.

1. "X" Section will relieve "Z" Section at "A" Battery position on the morning of the 8th inst.
   (a) Battery Commander Lt. A. K. STEEL.
   (b) "X" Section will leave Coy Hdqrs at 5.30. a.m.

2. Tripods and belt boxes will be handed over.

3. O.C. "Z" Section will hand over to O.C. "X" Section. All maps, Battery charts, Standing orders, and Trench Stores. Receipts will be sent to Hdqrs.

4. Relief complete will be wired to Headquarters. Code word "POPOUT".

5. "X" and "Z" Sections to acknowledge.

<u>Issued at 12.30. p.m.</u>

W. Hutho Capt/Major.
Commanding 254th M.G. Coy.

Copy No 1. to "X" Section.
  "   " 2 - "Z" Section.
  "   " 3 - "W" Section
  "   " 4 - "Y" Section   } for information.
  "   " 5 - D.M.G.O. 49th Div.
  "   " 6 - 146th Inf Bgde.
  "   " 7 - War Diary
  "   " 8 - Spare.

254th Machine Gun Company
Operation Order No. 19.

SECRET.   Copy No. 7.

Ref. Map. Sheet 28. 1/40.000.   11th January 1918.

1. The Company will be relieved by the 202nd Machine Gun Company on the morning of the 12th inst.
   (a). One Section 202nd M.G. Company will relieve Nos. 90. 91. 92 and 93 gun positions.
   (b). One Section 202nd M.G. Company will relieve "A" Battery.

2. One guide for each of Nos 90. 91. 92 and 93 guns, and two guides for "A" Battery will be provided from Headquarters, and will meet the Sections of the 202nd M.G. Company at BELGIAN BATTERY CORNER. H.24.a.20.45. at 5.0.a.m. on the 12th inst.

3. The following will be handed over by Sections in the Line:-
   - Tripods.
   - Belt boxes.
   - S.A.A.
   - Grenades.
   - Trench Pumps.
   - Beatrice Stoves.
   - Hot food Containers.
   - T. Bases.
   - Aiming Posts.
   - Picks and Shovels.
   - Standing Orders.
   - Maps and Barrage charts.

   Receipts for the above will be sent to Headquarters immediately after relief.

4. All details of work in hand or projected will be explained and shewn on the ground by the Officers concerned to the relieving Officers of the 202nd M.G. Company.

5. Relief complete will be wired to D.M.G.O. and Company Headquarters. Code word "YARD."

6. Acknowledge.

   Issued at 4.0. p.m.

                        S. Jas Haskins, Major.
                        Commanding 254th M.G. Coy.

   Copy No. 1. to "W" Section.
      "   "   2   "   "X" Section.
      "   "   3   "   "Y" Section.
      "   "   4   "   "Z" Section.
      "   "   5   "   202nd M.G. Coy.
      "   "   6   "   D.M.G.O. 49th Div.
      "   "   7   "   War Diary.
      "   "   8   "   Spare.

7.

Training Programme for the week ending 19th January 1918.

Date	Unit	Location of Training Ground	Nature of Training	Remarks
15.1.18.	254. M.G.C.	CHESTRE W.D.C.S.1.	Cleaning & Re-equipping	Afternoon devoted to Recreational Training.
16.1.18.	"	"	3 hours Gun work. 3/4 hr Infantry Drill & Rifle exercises.	
17.1.18.	"	"	3 hours Gun work. 1 hour Saluting Drill. 1/2 hour P. Training.	
18.1.18.	"	"	Route March.	
19.1.18.	"	"	1 1/2 hrs Gun work. 1 1/2 " Infantry Drill. 1/2 hour P. Training.	

.... Major.
Commanding 254 M.G.Coy.

Training Programme for the week ending 26th January 1918.

Date	Unit	Location of Training Ground.	Nature of Training.	Remarks
21.1.18.	254. M.G.C.	CAESTRE. M. 2. c. 8. 1.	½ hour P. Training 2½ hrs. Gun work. 1. hour Infantry Drill.	Afternoon devoted to Recreational Training.
22.1.18	"	"	½ hour. P. Training. 2½ hrs. Gun work. 1 hr. Rifle exercises & Squad Drill.	Firing on 30 yds Range if an allotment of the Range at BORRE can be obtained.
23.1.18	"	"	Route March. CAESTRE – ST SYLVESTRE CAPPEL – STEENVOORDE – EECKE – CAESTRE STATION.	
24.1.18.	"	"	½ hour P. Training. Section Tactical Scheme. 4. M. Guns with Vanguard Battn. of a Brigade Advanced Guard.	
25.1.18.	"	"	½ hour P. Training 2½ hours Gun work. 1 hour Infantry Drill.	
26.1.18.	"	"	½ hour P. Training. 1½ hour Saluting Drill. Interior Economy & Rifle exercises Kit Inspections &c.	

Geo. Hackin. MAJOR.
Commanding 254 M.G. Coy.

Training Programme for the week ending 2nd February 1918.

Date	Unit	Location of Training Ground.	Nature of Training.	Remarks
28.1.18.	254. M.G.C.	CAESTRE. W.2.c.8.1.	2½ hours Gun work. 1 hour Infantry Drill. One Section Firing. ½ hour P. Training.	Afternoon devoted to Recreational Training.
29.1.18.	"	"	2½ hours Gun work. 1 hour Infantry Drill. One Section on Range. ½ hour P. Training.	
30.1.18	"	"	Route March. CAESTRE - FLETRE - STRAZEELE PRADELLES - BORRE - L'HOFFAND LA KREULE - ST SYLVESTRE CAPPEL CAESTRE. One hour halt at LA KREULE.	
31.1.18	"	"	2½ hours Gun work. 1 hour Infantry Drill. One Section on Range.	
1.2.18.	"	"	BARRAGE SCHEME.	
2.2.18.	"	"	1½ hours Infantry Drill. Kit Inspection &c.	

Jas. Archer Major
Commanding 254. M.G. Coy.

Vol 5

WAR DIARY
of the
254th MACHINE GUN COMPANY.
for
FEBRUARY. 1918.

Sheet No. 1.

Army Form C. 2118.

WAR DIARY
or
INTELLIGENCE SUMMARY. 254th Machine Gun Company
(Erase heading not required.)

Instructions regarding War Diaries and Intelligence Summaries are contained in F.S. Regs., Part II. and the Staff Manual respectively. Title pages will be prepared in manuscript.

Place	Date	Hour	Summary of Events and Information	Remarks and references to Appendices
CAESTRE	1/2.2.18		Training as per programme III	III
W.2.c.8.1.	3/8.2.18		" " " " " IV	IV
"	9.2.18		(do). Lt. T.H. BURNIE proceeded on Course 2nd Army Central Sch. WISQUES (9.2.18-17.3.18)	
"	10.2.18		" " " " "	
"	11.2.18		Training as per programme V. Lt.H.R. HESKETH proceeded on Course P.&P.T. St. Pol.	V
"	12/14.2.18		" " " " "	
"	15.2.18		" " " " MAJOR S.C. HASKINS. M.C. " " M.G. Branch of the G.H.Q. Small Arms Sch.	
"	16.2.18		" " " " "	
"	17/19.2.18		" " " " VI	VI
"	20.2.18		Divisional Inter-Coy. Football Tournament. Played Semi-final at ZUITPEENE.	
"	21.2.18		Entrained at CAESTRE 4.0.p.m. Detrained at YPRES at 5.30.p.m.
			Moved to I.8.d.6.6. Sheet 28. (HORNE WORKS).	
			Interviewed O.C. 5th N.Z. M.G. Coy. Issued Operation Order No. 20.	20.
			Orders received for Major S.C. HASKINS. M.C. to proceed to 40th Division.	
I.8.d.6.6.	22.2.18		Relieved 5th N.Z. M.G. Coy. O.C. reconnoitred positions with O.C. N.Z. Coy.	
			"W" Section relieved Nos. 17. 18. 19. and 20. gun positions. "Z" Section relieved	

Sheet No. 2.

Army Form C. 2118.

WAR DIARY
or
INTELLIGENCE SUMMARY. — 254th Machine Gun Company
(Erase heading not required.)

Place	Date	Hour	Summary of Events and Information	Remarks and references to Appendices
I 8. A. 6. b.	22.2.18		Nos. 21. 22. 23 and 24 positions. Casualties NIL.	
"	23.2.18		Work on Camps. Quiet day in the line. Enemy activity below normal. Casualties NIL.	
"	24.2.18		Guns fired 3000 rounds on indirect Targets. Trench Mortars active on Section Dug-outs. Casualties NIL.	
"	25.2.18		Several parties of enemy seen by telescope, but all out of M.G. range. Harassing fire on indirect targets. Casualties NIL.	
"	26.2.18		"X" and "Y" Sections relieved "W" and "Z" in the line.	21.
"	27.2.18		Moved to CAFE BELGE AREA to MOUTOR LINES. H. 30. a. 3. 9. Sheet 28 along with other M.G. Coys. of the 49th Division pending the formation of Machine Gun Battalion.	
"	28.2.18		Nos. 17. 18. 19. 20. Guns fired on S.O.S. lines in conjunction with Artillery. This was on account of information received from a deserter that an attack was imminent on our trenches W. of POLDERHOEK. CHATEAU J.16. Section PILL BOXES were shelled Chiefly with A. 23 but no attack developed.	

III

Training Programme for the week ending 2nd February 1918.

Date	Unit	Location of Training Ground	Nature of Training	Remarks
28.1.18	254 M.G.Coy.	CAESTRE M.G.C.B.I.	Platoon Commands. 1 hour Infantry Drill. One Section firing 12 hour P.T.	Afternoon devoted to Recreational Training.
29.1.18	"	"	1½ hours Gun work. 1 hour Infantry Drill. One Section on Range. 1 hour P.T. Training.	
30.1.18	"	"	Route March. CAESTRE - FLETRE - STRAEELE - PRADELLES BURRE - L'HOFFLAND - LA KREULE - ST SYLVESTRE - CAPPEL - CAESTRE. One hour half of La Kreule	
31.1.18	"	"	1½ hours Gun work. 1 hour Infantry Drill. One Section on Range.	
1.2.18	"	"	BARRAGE SCHEME.	
2.2.18	"	"	1½ hours Infantry Drill. Kit Inspection &c.	

Commanding 254 M.G.Coy.

IV

Training Programme for the week ending 9th February 1918.

Date	Unit	Location of Training School	Action of Training.	Remarks
4.2.18.	254. M.G. Coy.	CAESTRE W. 2.c.8.1.	2½ hour Gun work. 1 hour Infantry Drill. 1 Section on Range.	Afternoons devoted to Recreational Training.
5.2.18	"	"	Barrage Drill. ½ hour Infantry Drill. ½ " P. Training.	
6.2.18	"	"	ROUTE MARCH.	
7.2.18.	"	"	2½ hour Barrage Drill. ½ hour Infantry Drill. 1 hour Stoppages. ½ " P. Training.	
8.2.18	"	"	Barrage Drill.	
9.2.18.	"	"	½ hour Infantry Drill. Belt filling.	

White Capt.

Training Programme for the week ending 16.2.1918.

Date	Unit	Location of Parade Ground	Nature of Training	Remarks
11.2.18	254 M.G.C.	CAESTRE M.2.c.8.1. — 30 yds. Range A1.W.7.a.1.7.	2½ hrs. Lewis Gun work. ½ " Infantry Drill. ½ " Lecture. ½ " P.T.	Firing to take place on 30 yds. Range on Thursday, Friday & Thursday. Lecture on Shoot 9 Th. & Fri. 1st
12.2.18	"	"	2½ hrs. Lewis Gun work. ½ to Infantry Drill. ½ " Lecture. ½ " P.T. & Bayonet.	
13.2.18	"		ROUTE MARCH CAESTRE - FLETRE - STRAZEELE - PRADELLES - BURRE - L'HOFFLAND - LA KREULE - ST SYLVESTRE CAPPEL - CAESTRE. (Lunch halt at LA KREULE)	
14.2.18	"		9.15 a.m. - 10.15 a.m. Sergeants Lecture. 10.15 " - 11.15 " Box Respirator Drill. 11.15 " - 12.15 p.m. Infantry Drill (extending movements). 4½ hrs. Lecture. ½ " P.T. & Bayonet.	
15.2.15	"		9.0 a.m - 1.0 p.m. Medical Lecture.	
16.2.18	"		9.0 a.m. - 10.30 a.m. Infantry Drill. (½ hour Thursday)	That. to. Capt.

Training Programme for the week ending 23rd February 1918.

Date.	Unit.	Location of Training Ground.	Nature of Training.	Remarks.
18.2.18.	254th M.G.C.	CAESTRE W.2.c.8.1.	9.a.m–10.a.m Infantry Drill & Musketry. 10. " – 1.p.m. Tactical Scheme.	During inclement weather, training in the open will be replaced by Gun work & tactics in Billets.
19.2.18.	"	30 yards Range W.7.c.1.7.	9.a.m–10.a.m Infantry Drill (including Musketry). 10. " – 11. " Gun Drill. 11. " – 12 noon. Mechanism. 12.noon–1.0.p.m. Immediate Action. 2.30.p.m.–3.0. " P. Training.	One Section on Range on Friday & Saturday.
20.2.18.	"	"	9.a.m – 1.p.m. Tactical Scheme.	Afternoons devoted to Recreational Training.
21.2.18.	"		8.0.a.m. Route March. CAESTRE – FLETRE – GODEWAERSVELDE STEENVOORDE – ST SYLVESTRE (APPEL).	
22.2.18.			9.a.m–10.a.m. Infantry Drill (& how Musketry). 10. " – 11. " Overhead fire drill. 11. " – 12.30.p.m. Stoppages. 12.30.p.m.–1.0. " Lecture. 2.30. " – 3.0.p.m. P. Training.	
23.2.18.			9.a.m.–10.30.a.m Saluting Drill & Musketry. 10.30. " – 11.30. " Mechanism. Billets. Kit Inspections. &c.	Thos S. Capt.

254th Machine Gun Company.
Operation Order No. 20.

SECRET
Ref. Map. Sheet 28. 1/40.000.

Copy No.
21st February 1918.

1. The Company will relieve the 5th New Zealand Machine Gun Company in the line on the 22nd inst.

    (a) "W" Section will relieve No. 1 Section 5th New Zealand Machine Gun Company in Nos. 16, 17, 18, and 19 gun positions.

    "Z" Section will relieve No. 2 Section 5th N.Z. Machine Gun Company in Nos. 20, 21, 22, & 23 gun positions.

    (b) "W" and "Z" Sections will leave Headquarters at 12 noon & will meet guides from 5th N.Z. Machine Gun Company at that hour at I.8.d.6.6.

2. Tripods, Belt boxes, and Trench stores will be handed over, the receipts being sent to Headquarters immediately after relief.

3. O.C. "W" Section and O.C. "Z" Section will take over all Maps, Standing Orders, and details of work relative to their gun positions.

4. Two filled belt boxes will be carried in by each gun team.

5. Relief complete will be wired to D.M.G.C. and Company Headquarters. Code word "NATURAL".

6. Acknowledge.

Issued at 9.30. p.m.

White Capt.
Commanding 254th M.G. Coy.

Copy No. 1. to "W" Section.
" " 2. " "Z" "
" " 3. " Transport Officer
" " 4. " 5th N.Z. M.G. Coy.
" " 5. " D.M.G.C. 49th Div. } For information.
" " 6. " "Y" Section.
" " 7. " "X" "
" Nos. 8 & 9. War Diary.
" No. 10. Spare.

254th Machine Gun Company.
Operation Order No. 21.

SECRET   Copy No. 9.

Ref. Map. Sheet 28. 1/40,000.

1. The following inter section reliefs will take place on the 26th inst:-
   (a) "X" Section will relieve "W" Section in Nos. 17. 18. 19. and 20 gun positions.
       "Y" Section will relieve "Z" Section in Nos. 21. 22. 23. and 24 gun positions.
   (b) "X" and "Y" Sections will leave Hqrs. at 7.30. a.m.
   (c) Guides will be provided from Headquarters.

2. Tripods & belt boxes will be handed over, but each gun team of "X" and "Y" Sections will carry in two belt boxes, & each gun team of "W" and "Z" Sections will carry out two belt boxes.

3. "W" and "Z" Sections will hand over to "X" and "Y" Sections all maps, charts, firing programmes and information concerning their positions.
   Receipts to be handed into Hdqrs. on completion of relief.

4. Relief complete will be wired to Hdqrs. Code word "JACKPOT".

5. "X" and "Y" Sections to acknowledge.

Issued at 4.0. p.m.

                         White Capt.
                     Commanding 254th M.G. Coy.

Copy No. 1. to "X" Section.
"   "   2. " "Y"   "
"   "   3. " "W"   "
"   "   4. " "Z"   "
"   "   5. " Transport Officer.
"   "   6. " D.M.G.C. ——— For information.
"   Nos. 7 & 8. War Diary.
"   No. 9.   Spare.

www.ingramcontent.com/pod-product-compliance
Lightning Source LLC
Chambersburg PA
CBHW081246170426
43191CB00037B/2054